WHAT'S NEXT?

WHAT'S NEXT?

A MILITARY VETERAN'S GUIDE
TO MAXIMIZING YOUR MBA

MATTHEW COWSERT

ISBN-13:978-1-7324312-1-8 | Paperback

ISBN-13:978-1-7324312-0-1 | eBook

To my wife Chelsea and son Jackson: Your unconditional love inspires me to be my best self every single day.

CONTENTS

PREFACE

I am writing this to increase the probability of success for veterans who are transitioning from active duty to earn an MBA before re-entering the civilian workforce. While this book will be most useful for aspiring MBA student veterans, there are tools that all MBA candidates can use to find their next careers.

I cannot explain my motivation for business school without mentioning my father, John T Cowsert. In my youth, he was the hardass, recently separated former Marine focused on ensuring that I was a productive (and well-behaved) citizen. Every chore, report card and athletic game was followed up by, **"Did you do your best?"** Honest to a fault, I always answered with a firm "no" and began to examine how to do better the next time. While I did not always appreciate it at the time, I credit my dad for helping cultivate my drive for constant self-improvement.

In high school and college, my dad was more focused on being there for me for games, graduations and life advice. Through our shared experiences and love of motorcycles, we developed the type of father-son friendship that others covet. Five months after watching me graduate from Ranger School, my dad, 47, unexpectedly passed away. I was devastated, and his death forced me into a period of profound introspection. It was during that time that my business-school journey began in earnest.

If I died tomorrow, would I be satisfied with what I had accomplished? Was I on track to achieve my personal and professional goals? What *are* my current goals? What should they be? How would I know when I found the right path?

While I loved my time in the Army, I knew in my heart it was never meant to be my long-term career. I needed to start planning my exit strategy. With four years left on my contract, I felt that I had time to figure it out. My plans were put on hold as I changed branches from infantry to finance, married my wife, Chelsea, and deployed to Afghanistan. Two years later, during that deployment, I began planning again.

My boss Sebastian was a Stanford graduate. He knew I had an undergraduate degree in accounting, so he recommended that I look into Stanford's business school for my grad school options. One of my main reasons for choosing the Army over another military branch was the opportunity to go to grad school on the Army's dime (GrADSO). I signed my contract in 2007, two years before the Post 9/11 G.I. Bill was in effect. As it was my only option for advanced education at the time, adding three years to my contract for free post-graduate education was appealing.

I grew up in a lower-middle-class household, living paycheck to paycheck. My undergraduate degree and Army commission finally provided the financial stability I dreamed of growing up. After reviewing the upfront costs and post-employment reports, the MBA route that Sebastian suggested seemed to offer the opportunity to increase my long-term financial stability.

While researching Stanford, I ran across a post that discussed "re-potting" your career. [1] The article used 10 years as the upper limit for staying engaged and innovative in a field. It struck a nerve, and I realized that I was dangerously close to my 10-year limit (including my undergraduate time at The Citadel, a senior military college in South Carolina).

I spoke with Chelsea about my realization, and she was supremely supportive. We had an honest conversation about the type of life that we wanted for our future family. Having both grown up in military households, we felt comfortable evaluating the pros and cons of each approach. It boiled down to one question: Did I think I had what it takes to transition successfully? Ultimately, I decided to bet on myself, a decision I have never regretted.

In fear of retribution from career officers who might not have agreed with my decision, I kept it to myself that I was going to use the Post 9/11 G.I. Bill. However, I made transitioning from the Army my singular focus. I knew I wanted a new career, but "not Army" was not the goal. I began exploring in more detail what options an MBA would provide.

I envisioned running my own business after the Army, so I started reading books about entrepreneurship. I found a book co-authored by Clayton M. Christensen called "How Will You Measure Your Life?". Reading that book was another seminal moment in my life. I began to think about my future career as Clay described it, a "job to be done." The only problem was that I did not know what kind of business I wanted to start.

---

[1] https://www.gsb.stanford.edu/insights/it-time-repot-your-career.

Around that same time, I received advice from a few veterans at the University of California, Haas School of Business who had recently visited Andreessen Horowitz, the venture capital firm. The partners there recommended that aspiring veteran entrepreneurs go to a reputable tech firm first, and then become an entrepreneur. That advice resonated, so entrepreneurship became my long-term goal (no longer my short-term aspiration) as I focused on tech careers in which I could acquire the skills and credibility to run a firm.

I also began scouring the internet for resources and found the veteran-to-MBA landscape to be barren,except for a few admission consultants and blogs. The advice boiled down to getting into the best program that you can, and starting early. While those were sound recommendations, they seemed incomplete. In response to the scarcity of information for transitioning veterans, I began compiling and adapting tools to augment my decision-making. I have since passed on those tools to veterans and non-veterans in my network, who have used them to achieve their goals.

I am going to share with you the advice and frameworks I developed to take me from a transitioning veteran to a successful student with an offer to work at one of the largest tech firms in the world. If I can do it, I am confident you can too. There are no silver bullets for long-term prosperity, but this book will help bring you one step closer to realizing your ideal future.

PART I: CONVINCE YOURSELF

Pre-Separation Instructions

CHAPTER 1: CAREER CONSIDERATIONS

The starting point of all achievement is desire.
—Napoleon Hill

Joining the military requires intestinal fortitude and a desire to push your natural limits. These qualities are part of what will set you apart from your peers. A successful transition from the military for an aspiring student veteran is not straightforward, as most military transition resources are not focused on student veterans. [2] Using an MBA as a segue between your military service and re-entering the workforce allows you to orient yourself to new career possibilities before signing another employment agreement. Veterans with MBAs are among the most marketable and attractive job candidates for employers.

To be clear: No one owes you anything. As with anything in life, there is a direct correlation between the effort you put into business school and your outcome. Will you receive support from other veterans along the way? Absolutely. Will your target schools have veteran enrollment

---

[2] I still remember being forced to apply to the post-separation jobs, even with my admissions letter in-hand from a top MBA program. Go figure!

goals? They will. Will your target firms have diversity-hiring initiatives? [3] You bet. These advantages are not guarantees. Assume you are the one veteran who is not a shoo-in and that you are going to have to put in extra effort to achieve your goals.

You will meet student veterans who span the spectrum from helpful to ineffectual. You will encounter schools that do not think you can make the transition to your target post-MBA career. [4] Some firms will hire you to work only within the same area you worked in while in the military. Despite all that, you will not find a better return on your investment than a top-tier (for you) MBA. We will dive deeper into how to evaluate the right school for you in Chapter 2.

The rest of this chapter will cover:

- Identifying and leveraging your strengths.
- Defining your goals.
- Evaluating your available paths with an MBA.
- How to decide what do you not want to do.
- Why finding your passion is not your goal.
- Tying up loose ends.

Identifying and Leveraging Strengths

Growing up, you may have heard that the path to success is to focus on shoring up your weaknesses. When transitioning from the military to earn an MBA, leveraging your strengths is the best approach.

Introspection is necessary if you want to make the most of your transition opportunities. If you already know your strengths and how to make them work for you, you should still take the time to validate

---

[3] Veterans are considered diversity hires.
[4] Your story or stats are not congruent with their archetype of a successful MBA.

your self-assessment with external tools and the assessments of your co-workers, friends and family.

Qualitative: Self
At a minimum, your self-reflection should include:

- Reverse-engineering your military evaluations to see what stands out. What trends emerge?
- Identifying the last project you worked with which you were so absorbed, you lost track of time.
- Reflecting what skills and tasks others praise you for or about which they seek your expertise. [5]

Qualitative: Others
These questions are always awkward to ask (it feels like fishing for compliments), but they are essential. Incorporate your mandatory 360-degree assessment feedback as well. At a minimum, you should ask:

- What do you view as my key strengths and attributes?
- What unique things do I bring to a team dynamic?
- Can you describe a time when you have seen me at my best?
- Can you describe a time when you have seen me at my worst?
- Where can I improve?

Cast a wide net and do not seek only the advice of those you know will praise you. A large sample size will bring to the surface your primary traits. Share your highlights with the outside world, through the stories you tell during your transition (applications and interviews). Work on your deficiencies internally and do your best to avoid putting

---

[5] https://www.themuse.com/advice/4-ways-to-figure-out-what-youre-good-at-not-just-what-youre-passionate-about.

yourself in situations, environments or jobs that stimulate those sub-optimal behaviors.

Quantitative

From experience, I recommend the CliftonStrengths assessment which will shed light on what you do best. Gallup's book "StrengthsFinder 2.0" comes with an access code for the assessment and gives you an individual Strengths Insight and Action-Planning Guide. Another book by Gallup, "Strengths Based Leadership", takes the results of your assessment and aligns your top strengths with the four domains of leadership (executing, influencing, relationship building, and strategic thinking). If you have already taken the assessment, there is no need to retake it, but if you start with "Strengths Based Leadership", it comes with an access code as well.

Each book provides different insights into your inherent strengths, with tools and advice for maximizing your abilities. If you find another strength assessment you want to try, go for it. What matters is that you have a tool to assess yourself.

By combining your qualitative and quantitative assessments, you are opening a window into careers in which you will thrive post-transition.

Defining Goals

A useful approach is to start at the end (10 years out) and work your way back to the present. From the perspective of persuading your target program to admit you and your target company to hire you, planning longer than 10 years from the start of your MBA program is nothing more than a guess. As you get closer to the present day, your goals need to be more specific.

For example, let us say you want to own and operate a technology consulting business (10-year goal). What skills and experiences do you have that indicate you can run your own business? What skills and experiences are you lacking? Consider how an MBA will help develop the skills you need, and how your short-term, post-MBA career will give you the experiences and credibility you need to achieve your long-term goal.

Now is the time to leverage your backward planning skills. Ensure congruence between the MBA curriculum (each school will have different resources, opportunities, and networks), your short-term goal, and your long-term goal. Define a path that is easy to communicate and supports your goals.

S.M.A.R.T.
At a micro-level, breaking each goal into sub-goals will improve your chance of success. The S.M.A.R.T. framework is a systematic way to approach each goal and is the civilian equivalent of having a task, purpose, and timeframe. [6] S.M.A.R.T. stands for:

- **Specific** (simple, sensible, significant).
- **Measurable** (meaningful, motivating).
- **Achievable** (agreed upon, attainable).
- **Relevant** (realistic, resourced, and results-based).
- **Time-bound** (time-based, time-limited, time-sensitive).

Example short-term goal
Evaluate each target school for "fit."

---

[6] https://www.mindtools.com/pages/article/smart-goals.html.

Example S.M.A.R.T goal
Specific: Evaluate Stanford, Haas, and Sloan business schools.
Measurable: Evaluate each program according to your program criteria matrix. [7]
Achievable: Reach out to current students at Stanford, Haas, and Sloan, attend their webinars and visit their campuses.
Relevant: Evaluate the increase or decrease in the certainty (from your interactions) that Stanford, Haas, Sloan support your short-term and long-term goals before writing essays.
Time-bound: Within 90 days, 30 days for each school.

Do not be surprised if your initial goals (target career or program) change as you gather information. As you compare your assumptions with the uncovered facts, your target program and future career lists will naturally get smaller.

Evaluating Available MBA Paths

There are many options for U.S. MBA programs. Two years or one? Part-time or full-time? Online or in person? Top school or the school offering you the most money?

For most veterans, a full-time, in person MBA program makes the most sense. Choosing the more extended program increases your opportunities to demonstrate competency to potential employers. Think about this in the context of what you are missing that your MBA classmates (your competition for jobs) already have?

While you may know MBA student veterans (and you should reach out to them), you do not have the type of business-focused network that your peers have to rely on during your internship and full-time recruiting efforts. Most of your professional network is still in the

---

[7] Discussed in more detail in Chapter 2.

military, with limited contacts or focus on your target industry. You need to build a professional network that you can depend on and contribute to later. Meaningful relationships take time to develop and are easier to cultivate in person.

You are a career-switcher, a characteristic you share with many of your MBA classmates. Evaluating industries takes time and building the skills and experiences necessary to land your dream role takes even longer. Your MBA will give you two years to prove your value to employers and increase your probability of success.

When evaluating your options, remove financial aid from your decision criteria (for now). It is counterintuitive, but from a return on investment perspective, scholarships and stipends are nominal. Your focus should be on the floor (salary right out of the MBA program) and the ceiling (expected salary with advancement). To illustrate this point, the figure below looks at two programs in the same city (removing basic allowance for housing as a consideration). School 1 is a top 10 program and School 2 is a top 50 program. We use four years after graduation because that is the traditional vesting timeline for restricted stock awards).

	T0	T1	T2	T3	T4	T5
School 1						
Total Cost of Attendance	$111,570	$111,570				
Financial Aid (loans)	58,765	58,765	(29,383)	(29,383)	(29,383)	(29,383)
Scholarship						
G.I. Bill	22,805	22,805				
Yellow Ribbon	30,000	30,000				
Salary	24,000	10,000	142,000	142,000	142,000	142,000
Bonus			55,000	45,000		
Stock			6,250	18,750	50,000	50,000
Cash Flows for Discounting	135,570	121,570	173,868	176,368	162,618	162,618
Terminal Value						1,506,462
Discount Factor	1.00	0.87	0.76	0.66	0.57	0.50
Discounted Cash Flows	135,570	105,713	131,469	115,964	92,977	829,827
Net Present Value	**$1,411,521**					

Figure 1-1. Net present value calculations for School 1.

Figure 1-1 Explained

School 1 did not offer you any scholarships, but you can take advantage of the G.I. Bill and Yellow Ribbon Program for two years. Your salary includes your internship ($2,000 each week over 12 weeks) in the first year, your TA position ($10,000) in the second year, and your starting compensation for the first four years after graduation. Your bonus is split over the first two years ($55,000 up-front, $45,000 spread over 12 installments in the second year). Your stock compensation is backloaded (5% in the first year, 15% in the second, and 40% in the third and fourth year). The vesting schedule ensures incentive alignment; the longer you stay and contribute, the more you earn.

Now we will dig into the financial terms. This is an excellent opportunity to learn more about these terms in a personally meaningful way if you do not understand them. [8] Cash flows for discounting considers the time value of money (TVM) with the assumption that a dollar today is worth more than a dollar later. The terminal value is an estimate of your future cash flows, assuming perpetual growth. While directionally useful, it is not a calculation you should get hung up on, as projecting the future beyond period 5 (T5) is difficult. For example, in the sixth year you could get a promotion that offers 10 times your annual salary in the previous year, or you could start a business in the eighth year and not draw a paycheck for a few years.

The discount factor assumes a personal discount rate of 15%. A study conducted in the 1990s when the military was downsizing calculated the rate to be 17%. [9] When service members were given a choice between lump sums and annuities, they chose the lump sums so often

---

[8] I did not know them all before business school.
[9] https://www.jstor.org/stable/2677897?seq=1#page_scan_tab_contents

that they would have to earn 17% on the lump sums to break even with the annuities. If this topic is of interest to you, I recommend reading the Naval Postgraduate School paper, "Personal Discount Rates and Retirement Decisions: Evidence from the U.S. Military", by Lucas A. Francavilla. [10]

The discounted cash flows (DCF) are a representation of how much money you will earn in each period in today's dollars. Remember that T5 considers all periods beyond the fifth year (perpetual growth). We sum the value of the DCF across all periods to arrive at the net present value (NPV) of attending School 1. We are not focusing on the probability of landing this job. You can land the same job used in the School 1 example at School 2, but the likelihood of doing so is lower. The probability calculation is subjective (correlation does not equal causation), so we exclude it here. Simply recognize the opportunity frequency is different in each program.

	T0	T1	T2	T3	T4	T5
School 2						
Total Cost of Attendance	$77,585	$77,585				
Financial Aid (loans)						
Scholarship	$44,780	$44,780				
G.I. Bill	$22,805	$22,805				
Yellow Ribbon	$10,000	$10,000				
Salary	$18,000	$10,000	$90,000	$95,000	$105,000	$110,000
Bonus			$20,000	$25,000	$25,000	$35,000
Stock						
Cash Flows for Discounting	$95,585	$87,585	$110,000	$120,000	$130,000	$145,000
Terminal Value						$1,137,692
Discount Factor	1.00	0.87	0.76	0.66	0.57	0.50
Discounted Cash Flows	95,585	76,161	83,176	78,902	74,328	637,725
Net Present Value	**$1,045,876**					

Figure 1-2. Net present value calculations for School 2.

---
[10]
https://calhoun.nps.edu/bitstream/handle/10945/49609/13Jun_Francavilla_Lucas.pdf?

When comparing the two options, school 1 provides a higher NPV (plus $365,000) because of the opportunity to earn more post-graduation. That more than makes up having to pay out of pocket $117,000 for School 1 while School 2 (Figure 1-2) was free.

To get most out of the analysis, ensure that you are comparing the post-employment career opportunities in your target industry, not the school's average. You do not want to think your average salary upon graduation will be $125,000 when it is actually $100,000 for the career you are pursuing. The salary figures in the School 2 model are estimates, as each school breaks down compensation differently, but the point is that *financial aid should not dictate your decision.* [11]

You should be more focused on the question: "Is this program (business school), from this school (larger university ecosystem) going to provide me the best platform to accomplish my goals?" You want to ensure that you make an apples-to-apples comparison. A proxy for parity is the post-MBA job opportunities statistic. [12] If the opportunities are the same, add back the financial aid offerings.

What Do You Not Want to Do?

You should focus on eliminating all the career trajectories that you do not want. Read about being a consultant, investment banker, "insert career that requires an MBA" and decide for yourself if the experiences, opportunities, and lifestyles described are consistent with what you want from a post-military life. [13] Also, when you have career vetting discussions with industry professionals, ensure that you dig for meaningful insights in their attitude and demeanor. The more you

---

[11] Available for download from my website to help in your decision-making.
[12] Available on most MBA programs' websites or by email request.
[13] Recommended starting points listed under Resources on nextvets.com.

whittle down your list of potential careers, the more clarity you will have when evaluating your target schools.

Figures 1-3 – 1-5 are examples of career matrices you can adapt to your needs. [14] The criteria listed are the components I was looking for in my next career. Everyone's consideration will be unique, but I will quickly walk through my thinking here.

- Listed criterion.
- Allocated weights (needs to total to 100%; do not change across industry).
- Gave each criterion a rating from -3 to +3 (higher is better).

I wanted a career that leveraged my strengths. That was most important to me. I did not want frequent travel to be a part of my life. I have a wife and son, and I enjoy seeing them for dinner. I wanted to work with exceptional people who challenged me to get better every day. Work-life balance is important to me, but if I'm engaged at work, this is a non-issue. Career advancement opportunities and financial rewards were necessary, but not my primary drivers. Lastly, I decided that location mattered to me. After spending time at Fort Irwin in California and then in Hawaii, I knew that my post-graduation location would make a material difference to my happiness.

Come up with your list, and then use it when you are learning more about each profession (for example, books, websites and informational interviews). Being deliberate about what attributes of your life you care about most after the military will make it more likely to find a career that has those attributes. Once you have decided on an industry, use the matrix to evaluate the companies within that

---

[14] Available for download from nextvets.com.

industry. You may be surprised to find a large amount of variance within an industry.

Consulting: Career Criteria Matrix			
Criteria	**Score**	**Weight**	**Adjusted**
1 Leverages my strengths	2	.30	.60
2 Regular travel	-2	.20	(.40)
3 Work with exceptional peers	3	.15	.45
4 Work / life balance	2	.05	.10
5 Opportunity for advancement	3	.10	.30
6 Financially rewarding	3	.10	.30
7 Located in cities I want to live	1	.10	.10
	Total	100%	**1.45**

Figure 1-3. My consulting career criteria matrix. View all careers through the same criteria for consistent comparisons across industries.

Investment Banking: Career Criteria Matrix			
Criteria	**Score**	**Weight**	**Adjusted**
1 Leverages my strengths	1	.30	.30
2 Regular travel	2	.20	.40
3 Work with exceptional peers	3	.15	.45
4 Work / life balance	-3	.05	(.15)
5 Opportunity for advancement	3	.10	.30
6 Financially rewarding	3	.10	.30
7 Located in cities I want to live	3	.10	.30
	Total	100%	**1.90**

Figure 1-4. My investment banking career criteria matrix.

Product Management: Career Criteria Matrix			
Criteria	**Score**	**Weight**	**Adjusted**
1 Leverages my strengths	3	.30	.90
2 Regular travel	3	.20	.60
3 Work with exceptional peers	3	.15	.45
4 Work / life balance	1	.05	.05
5 Opportunity for advancement	3	.10	.30
6 Financially rewarding	3	.10	.30
7 Located in cities I want to live	2	.10	.20
	Total	100%	**2.80**

Figure 1-5. My product management career criteria matrix.

Find Your Passion?

Most advice you see as you search for career transition advice focuses on "finding your passion." It is admirable to pursue your passion if you know what it is but finding your passion is another matter.

Your immediate focus should not be on finding your passion. First, the likelihood that you are going to have the time and perspective to find it during your transition is low. Second, most life's passions are not money-making endeavors and will continue to evolve with your experiences and motivations.

Dan and Chip Heath, in "The Power of Moments: Why Certain Experiences Have Extraordinary Impact", succinctly explain that "purpose trumps passion." Finding your purpose is a better goal than finding your passion because you can share a purpose (with admissions committees, classmates, and recruiters), while passions are usually too specific to share with a larger audience. Also, focusing on your next purpose opens multiple doors to reaching it.

Finding a career that matches your strengths will increase the likelihood of your career having purpose. The confidence you receive from being an expert in your field will permeate throughout your life. From a position of power, your career trajectory will accelerate. You can then invest your additional cash and credibility into opportunities and causes that you find meaningful. If you want to dig deeper into this topic, I recommend reading Cal Newport's "So Good They Can't Ignore You: Why Skills Trump Passion in the Quest for Work You Love".

Tying up Loose Ends
Do an Incredible Job in Your Current Role
Most of the stories that you will share with future employees will come from your previous two positions. Do your best to frame your accomplishments in a civilian-friendly way. You might as well get started translating your achievements. [15]

Re-engage With Your Previous Supervisors
Let them know you plan to attend business school and ask for their endorsement. Do not tell your current boss yet, or risk having business-school pursuit used against you for the rest of your service.

Get Your VA paperwork in Order
If you have a disability claim to file, getting your supporting documentation, follow-up assessments, and referrals are easier to do while you are on active duty. Also, enroll for your G.I. Bill benefits. Your transition briefings will cover the enrollment process in depth. Once you receive your G.I. Bill Certificate of Eligibility, send it to your school's certifying official.

---

[15] I fondly remember sitting down with my HR manager to explain what "design thinking" was and why it was on my evaluation support form as a finance officer.

Check Your Separations Manual
Do not sign up for military schooling opportunities until you know whether they require an additional service commitment. Professional Military Education opportunities and Permanent Changes of Station usually require a one-year concurrent commitment upon arrival to your new duty station. Once you are accepted, you do not want to beg for a deferral.

Additional Considerations
It is OK if your post-MBA career does not end up matching what you write about in your applications; that is a common at business school. What you think you want to do in your post-MBA career is a direct reflection of your life experiences and understanding of the opportunities available to you. If you find a new opportunity along the way that meets your criteria and allows you to be the best version of yourself, do not be afraid to explore it.

"Plans are useless, but planning is indispensable," Dwight D. Eisenhower said. Throughout the planning process, you are going to learn a lot about yourself, but that is just the first step. In that spirit, we will now move on to the next part of the vetting process, evaluating what programs are right for you.

CHAPTER 2: RADICAL TRANSPARENCY

It's not about making the right
choice. It's about making a
choice and making it right.
—J.R. Rim

You now have the proper mindset to evaluate your target programs. At a minimum, you know what you do not want to do. You are about to enter a lifelong partnership. To make the right decision for you, your eyes need to be wide open.

A Quick Note on Rankings

Rankings serve a purpose, at least as a signaling tool to prospective students and employers. To do your due diligence, look at the criteria that each publication uses to determine its rankings.

Glenn Hubbard, Columbia Business School's dean, wrote the article "Do B-school rankings really matter?", in Fortune in 2015 and proposed an inputs-and-outputs approach for evaluating business schools. [16] The next day, the online publication Poets & Quants published "How a Dean Would Rank Business Schools", using

---

[16] http://fortune.com/2015/04/06/do-b-school-rankings-really-matter/?

Hubbard's method and gave a transparent breakdown for each input and output. [17] If you are looking for objectivity in ranking your target programs, apply the same methodology using the most recently published data.

This section will cover:

- What you are buying with an MBA.
- The importance of geography and alumni.
- Program resources to explore at each school.

What Are You Buying?

The three immediate benefits of an MBA for you are:

- Access to jobs you would not be eligible for without an MBA.
- A lifelong, business-focused network.
- A flexible transition period from the military to the civilian workforce.

Job Access

Most jobs MBA candidates desire require an MBA. For veterans who do not have legitimate business experience before obtaining their MBAs, the degree will open doors that would otherwise stay closed. Even if you are qualified to work in a particular industry before your MBA, it will allow you to enter most firms at a higher level; for example, as an associate rather than an entry-level analyst.

Your job prospects have increased compared with peers who are making a direct transition from the military into the civilian workforce. However, understand that MBA candidates who stay in their career field will usually land the most coveted jobs in those fields because they are the most qualified applicants. For example, venture

---

[17] https://poetsandquants.com/2015/04/07/a-new-and-better-way-to-rank -the-best-business-schools/

capital firms are notoriously difficult to enter without relevant experience.

MBA programs are designed to provide you with opportunities for relevant experience in your areas of interest through semester internships, fellowships, and incubator programs. When engaging with each school, ask about the opportunities for exposure to your target industry.

You are always working to validate that your skills match your strengths. You do not need to have those skills currently but learning them should feel like a natural extension. For example, a career in venture capital requires a high level of detail-oriented due diligence and sophisticated financial modeling. If you excel in detail-oriented work and love financially analyzing companies, a VC role may right for you.

Business Network

Building your network is one of the most rewarding experiences that you will have as an MBA. Whether you realize it or not, you already have experience networking. Every time you coordinated with another unit to conduct a mission or training, you were networking. The "war story" that you told at your last military ball was networking. Building your MBA network is not much different. Take a genuine interest in your classmates' stories, motivations, and goals, and you will find that your network will grow without much effort.

Your classmates, professors, and external speakers will challenge your way of thinking and force you to consider new positions. As you get to know your new network, do not be afraid to ask for advice or introductions. Your new network wants to help you. Your success reflects well on them, too.

Flexibility

First, you are not pigeon-holing yourself into one career. You will find MBAs across most industries and functional areas. Second, depending on your transition status, G.I. Bill benefits, Yellow Ribbon contributions or scholarships, you are likely paying less for your education than your classmates. The reduced financial pressure will increase your options for post-MBA employment.

For example, if you decide to enter a career field that is initially low-paying compared with other industries you are not going to starve while paying down your student loans. You can also decide to start your own company or become a search-fund entrepreneur without going broke.

Geography and Alumni

The location of your target program will have a more substantial impact on your success than you realize. Schools in larger metropolitan areas (for example, New York, Boston or San Francisco) tap into the industries in their areas and are more expensive than their rural counterparts. It is easier to meet new people (dating) and own your outcome (like semester internships or networking outside of your MBA network for job opportunities) at urban schools. Programs in more rural areas force you to rely more on on-campus recruiting and relationships with alumni for employment opportunities. One is not inherently better than the other, but you need to have a clear understanding of your options when evaluating target schools.

You should also consider the location of alumni from your target programs. All schools collect this information, and it should be readily accessible from their websites. If you cannot find the information yourself, reach out to the career services office, and they can provide you with the information or let you know where you can get it. This information will give you a reasonable understanding of the power of the school's alumni network. Only a few MBA programs have worldwide recognition and appeal.

If you are dead set on living in a specific location, make sure that alumni from your target school live there. You do not want to miss the opportunities to leverage your network which you worked so hard to build. Your location post-graduation will influence your ability to tap into alumni (or as an alum, your ability to give back). The farther you travel from your school, expect a weaker alumni network (not including the clusters of alumni in prominent cities).

Program Resources

Let us looks at the resources that will have the most substantial impact on your application decision and your future. Use these resources to decide if a program is right for you. [18] We will break these down into:

- Current students.
- Industry connections.
- Professors and curriculum.
- Research centers and labs.

Current Students

The best way to measure your fit with a target school is to talk with current students. You can do this through in-person meetings, phone calls and email. Think about aspects of the MBA experience that you are most looking forward to and see if your expectations are consistent with their experiences. The more specific your questions are, the better feedback you will get from current students.

---

[18] Program criteria matrix.

For example, when speaking to second-year students, ask them how the curriculum helped them during their internships. Were there opportunities they took advantage of outside classes that helped them in their internships? Would they do it differently if they could do it again? Do not ask first-year students curriculum questions, because they have not had the opportunity to put their learnings into practice.

For connection starting points, look for students with things you have in common, like undergraduate school, branch of service and target industry. Veterans are valuable to meet during your evaluation period, but they should not be your only contacts. We will cover informational interview guidelines in Chapter 3.

Industry Connections
You are coming to business school to secure a career-accelerating job. What existing relationships are there between your target school and your target industry? MBA programs change regularly, so do not rely solely on school reputation. Programs known for banking and management consulting also have excellent technology and entrepreneurship programs, and many schools known for their entrepreneurial expertise have strong relationships with investment banks and management consulting firms.

Use the number of recent graduates in your area of interest as a proxy for success. Pull the employment reports for the past three to five years and see if you can find an increase or decrease in your area of interest.

If your target industry is in the top three already for the program, you are looking for steady state or growth (plus or minus three percent, year over year). A steady state shows that firms in that industry value students from the program. A regular year-over-year decline could be a signal that firms are not finding quality candidates from that program.

If your target industry is not in the top three already for the program, look for growth of three percent or more, year-over-year. If you do not see an increase in your target area of interest for that school, take a hard look at why you are attracted to the program. If you want to go to that school (and have an increased chance of admission), you may need to adjust your target role post-MBA.

Finding a less-well-known but exciting aspect of the program and highlighting it in your application essays will set you apart from your peers.

Professors and Curriculum

Each school you apply to will have professors, course structures, and schedules that are different from other schools. Think about the pros and cons of each approach. How do you learn best? How important is a four-day versus a five-day course load? Are you better at analyzing cases or experiential learning? Do the best professors teach during the day or in the evening? Are there opportunities to do joint research with professors you admire? What about being their teaching assistant? The variance in content you will receive from the top schools is small, but the difference in the delivery method will be significant. Explore and learn what matters most to you.

Research Centers and Labs

Each school is going to have research centers and labs around their areas of interest. These centers are where most of the intra-school collaborations take place, hosting entrepreneurship workshops, case competitions, and hackathons. These are the type of resources and opportunities you can use to differentiate yourself from your peers to employers.

Funding is available to pursue the best ideas, so if you want to start your own company, doing so while earning an MBA is a very low-risk way to see if your venture is valid. You want to move from business idea to viable business model as soon as possible, and these centers and labs are designed to help you do just that.

Best-case scenario: you receive funding from the school or local investment firms before you leave school.

Worst-case scenario: you use your failed experience as a learning point and use your initiative to land a steady job before graduation.

Summary

You should be excited at the possibilities ahead when researching programs. If you do not have a positive impression or feeling about a school, look for objective ways to evaluate your intuition. Was there a mismatch between your expectation and what the program offers? Did you have a positive or negative experience when visiting? Did the location of the school help or hurt your impression?

At this stage, you want to gather objective evidence for why these programs are great fits for you. Have you added or dropped criteria during your due diligence? If so, make sure to evaluate each school against the same standards. When deciding, you will end up using both objective and subjective evidence. The program criteria matrices in Figures 2-1 and 2-2 below are one way to evaluate each program. [19]

---

[19] Available for download from nextvets.com.

School 1: Program Criteria Matrix			
Criteria	**Score**	**Weight**	**Adjusted**
1 Current student interactions	1	.20	.20
2 Location	3	.15	.45
3 Within 80% range statistically	-1	.10	(.10)
4 Class size	3	.05	.15
5 Program structure	3	.15	.45
6 Target industry reputation	3	.10	.30
7 Target firm alumni presence	3	.10	.30
8 Exceptional Professors	3	.05	.15
9 Program Specific Opportunities	3	.05	.15
10 Financial Aid	0	.05	0
	Total	100%	**2.05**

Figure 2-1. Program criteria matrix for School 1.

School 2: Program Criteria Matrix			
Criteria	**Score**	**Weight**	**Adjusted**
1 Current student interactions	3	.20	.60
2 Location	3	.15	.45
3 Within 80% range statistically	1	.10	.10
4 Class size	3	.05	.15
5 Program structure	3	.15	.45
6 Target industry reputation	2	.10	.20
7 Target firm alumni presence	3	.10	.30
8 Exceptional Professors	3	.05	.15
9 Program Specific Opportunities	2	.05	.10
10 Financial Aid	3	.05	.15
	Total	100%	**2.65**

Figure 2-2. Program criteria matrix for School 2.

CHAPTER 3:
INFORMATIONAL
INTERVIEWS

What we plant in the soil of
contemplation, we shall reap in
the harvest of action.
—Meister Eckhart

There is no substitute for genuine human connection. For all the rigor that you put into your transition, you are still going to make a biased decision on where you go to school, and where you want to work (and that is OK). Think back on significant transitions in your life. How much did the first impression of the people you met at your new school, unit or neighborhood influence your attitude toward your future there?

The rigor you use to evaluate your future business school and career is not much different from any other evaluative process. The admissions committees are vetting you (application, interviews), and you are vetting them (to decide which program is right for you). Informational interviews will allow you to learn the difference between an opportunity worth taking and one you should pass on.

Informational interviews
We briefly mentioned informational interviews in Chapter 2, but we are now going to do a deep dive. Steve Dalton's "The 2-Hour Job Search", covers an interview method that excels for this stage of your search.

Your focus should be on current students at your target schools. Reach out both to veterans and non-veterans in your target industry.

TIARA

TIARA stands for Trends, Insights, Advice, Resources, and Assignments. The best part of this framework is that it is flexible, and not all informational interviews will require such diligence. Below is an example of TIARA in action.

Trends: I have heard that (X program) is known for placing graduates in (X industry). Have you noticed that trend or pattern among your classmates? Do see any emerging recruiting trends? (Trends can be an internship, full-time recruiting or diversity hiring initiatives.)

Insights: I know you were just in my shoes a year or so ago. What helped you determine that (X program) was the right school for you? What has surprised you since you have been in school? How do you feel that the MBA is helping you achieve your goals? What makes (X program) unique to you?

Advice: What can I be doing to be a competitive candidate and stand out? Is there anything you wish you had done earlier to get a jump-start in recruiting for (X industry)?

Resources: What resources would you recommend I investigate before applying (school or industry specific)? Who else should I connect with before applying?

Assignments: (Optional. Useful if you are speaking to a second year MBA student about their internship). Why did you decide to join X firm for the summer? What type of project did you work on? Were there any courses you took that first year that helped you? Were there any classes you wish you would have taken sooner? What did you think of the culture? Are you returning?

Using a version of this format will force you to be thoughtful about the types of questions you ask. Additionally, as you assess your different target schools, you can use the responses you collect as additional data points when deciding where you want to go to school.

CHAPTER 4: HOW AM I PAYING FOR THIS AGAIN?

Planning is bringing the future
into the present so that you can
do something about it now.
—Alan Lakein

You are the only person who knows how much money you will need to save to get you through the next few years. Here are a few factors to consider that will help you come to your conclusions.

How Much do You Need to Save?

While you should not base your decision solely on which school offers you the most money, you should have a clear picture of your financial situation with each offer you receive. Do everything you can to reduce your monthly spending before leaving active duty (like paying off your car and canceling unnecessary subscriptions). Save as much money as you can while you are on active duty. I left with $25,000 and wish I had saved more. Having six months of living expenses saved is ideal. Other considerations include:

Department of Veteran Affairs Augmentation

If you have 100% of the G.I. Bill, you are eligible for the Yellow Ribbon Program. Yellow Ribbon, run by the Department of Veteran Affairs, monetarily matches the amount specified by each school.

For example, a $10,000 per year Yellow Ribbon financial award (given by the school), is matched by the VA (through the Yellow Ribbon program), giving you an added $20K a year to pay for school. However, if you do not have 100% of the G.I. Bill benefits, you will not be eligible for the Yellow Ribbon program. If you cannot find what you are looking for on the VA website, contact the military veterans club at the schools you are considering. [20] Each club can provide a breakdown or put you in touch with the VA certifying official who will give an analysis of the amount and type of funding to expect.

Relationship Status

If you are married, you need to have more money saved to help finance the cost of supporting your family over the next two years. On the flipside, if your spouse is working while you are going to school, you will have to borrow less money. If your spouse is not working, expect to need more money saved for living expenses and healthcare. School healthcare premiums average an additional $5,000 a year and usually covers all dependents. Check with each program for specifics.

Total Cost of Attendance

The total cost of attendance is the maximum amount of money you can borrow to pay for your education (from banks or a 529 plan). The calculation assumes you are single and must pay for your housing. Scholarships and G.I. Bill / Yellow Ribbon awards count toward your total cost of attendance, but your Basic Allowance for Housing does not. Below, in Figure 4-1 is NYU Stern's total cost of attendance. The

---

[20] https://www.vets.gov/gi-bill-comparison-tool

numbers change incrementally every year, but this will give an idea of what you can expect to borrow.

2017-2018 Budget for MBA1 Students	
(Based on a nine-month academic year)	
NYU Stern Tuition & Fees	
Tuition	$69,086
Registration Fees*	$4,092
Living Expenses	
Room & Board	$25,320
Books & Supplies	$1,980
Transportation	$1,110
Miscellaneous**	$8,756
Loan Fees	$218
Total	**$110,562**
*Registration Fees includes a one-time fee of $1,520 for LAUNCH (Orientation)	
**Includes NYU Student Health Insurance costs	

Figure 4-1. Example total cost of allowance.

2017-2018 Budget for MBA1 Students	
(Based on a nine-month academic year)	
NYU Stern Tuition & Fees (with scholarship)	
Tuition	$0
Registration Fees	$0
Scholarship Stipend	($10,000)
Living Expenses	
Room & Board	$25,320
Books & Supplies	$1,980
Transportation	$1,110
Miscellaneous	$8,756
Loan Fees	$218
Eligible Borrowing Amount	**$27,384**

Figure 4-2. Example eligible borrowing amount.

The scholarship covers tuition. Your deposit covers registration fees. The stipend you get as a scholarship recipient reduces your overall ability to borrow. [21] The amount you can borrow is constant for federal and private student loan options. You will live off your eligible borrowing amount plus your Basic Allowance for Housing stipend. Anything you borrow beyond that amount will be as a separate personal loan and will carry a higher interest rate (usually 10% or higher).

Housing

Housing will be one of your most significant expenses during your MBA. If your circumstances allow it, finding a roommate will enable

---

[21] Worksheet available for download from nextvets.com.

you to live within your means much easier. Be honest about how much space you need. You will spend most of your time at school (club events, meetings, classes) and traveling during your breaks. Later in the year (after you have been admitted), there is usually a school-specific spreadsheet circulated listing soon to be available apartments from graduating second year MBA students. Such apartments are often available without using a real estate broker.

If you have a spouse, children, or pets, your situation will be different and expect to spend more of your housing allowance.

If you are moving to a large metropolitan area, you may need a real estate broker to find housing promptly. Broker fees can range from a few hundred to a few thousand dollars. Check with current students to see what to expect, and plan accordingly.

When Will You Receive Your Funding?

Your financial support will not all come at the same time. Understanding when to expect your money will allow you to plan for the times when you will not get any and prevent cash flow problems.

I will not cover the G.I. Bill / Yellow Ribbon payments to the school; you never see that money. Also, do not worry if the school is having issues with the VA paperwork or, for example, a government shutdown is looming. The school will give you the benefit of the doubt (eligibility to enroll in classes) as they work through the bureaucracy.

Basic Allowance for Housing

Your stipend will cover only your housing costs for the months that you are attending school (eight or nine months a year). The plus side is that you will have more of your G.I. Bill for further education. With the Harry W. Colmery Veterans Educational Assistance Act of 2017, there is no longer a restriction on how long you have to use your G.I.

Bill benefits. The only downside of not receiving the housing allowance all year is that you will have to pay out-of-pocket for housing when you are not in school.

To be clear, you get the allowance for the preceding month, so if you start school in September, you will not receive your first stipend until October. The benefit to this is that when you end your semester, you will get a payment the next month. At a minimum, have the money to cover your first month's rent and security deposit.

Book Stipend
The VA gives you a book stipend at the beginning of each semester. The amount varies based on the course load that you are taking. Expect between 60-70% of your stipend to hit your account during the first 30 days of your first semester and the remaining 30-40% to arrive in the second semester. The total amount caps at $1000 each year. Most MBA programs do not require expensive books, but it is an ancillary benefit.

Loan Disbursements
Loan disbursements are the only vehicle that gives you money before you need it. If you plan to use student loans, expect each payment about 10 days before the start of each semester.

If you have more questions, the best resource is the bursar at your school.

Semester Internships
Fall and spring semester internships can help offset the cost of going back to school. You can also work for the school in admissions, as a teaching assistant, or in some other capacity. School jobs are paid with tuition remittance, but if you are on a full scholarship the money will be paid to you directly throughout the semester.

What About Out-of-Pocket Expenses?

If financial aid does not cover all your tuition, the school will deduct the outstanding amount from your student loan disbursement, or you will need to write a check around the time you register for the next semester's classes.

Health Care Premiums

VA health care is free, and you can go to any VA facility for treatment. You need to file for it with the VA and send your certificate of coverage to the school before the school year begins. You cannot start the school year without coverage.

With school health care, you pay the premium, but the G.I. Bill reimburses the cost (through the school's bursar) to you during the semester. If you have dependents and use school health care, you will receive a partial reimbursement (for your premiums, not your dependents'). Health care premiums are due before you receive your loan disbursements, so plan accordingly.

PART II: CONVINCE TARGET SCHOOLS

From Stereotype to Archetype

CHAPTER 5: GMAT VS. GRE

Spectacular achievement is
always preceded by
unspectacular preparation.
—Robert H. Schuller

What happened to the days when you only had one entrance exam to hate? Which exam should you take? Here are the scenarios for when taking one over the other is preferable.

Target Degree

Are you pursuing a dual degree? If you are seeking a dual degree that is not a JD/MBA or MD/MBA, taking the GRE over the GMAT makes sense. The GRE allows you to prepare for one exam instead of two.

If you are not pursuing a dual degree, you are better off taking the GMAT. The quantitative section of the GMAT is more difficult and indicative of your coursework than the quant section of the GRE. An 80% quant score on the GMAT is not equal to an 80% quant score on the GRE.

Target Industry

You thought the evaluations stopped after admissions? The truth is that many firms request your GMAT or GRE scores during the summer internship and full-time application process. Some firms ask only for your GMAT, which means that if you took the GRE to get into school, you now need to take and do well on the GMAT to be competitive. GMAT requests are most relevant for consulting and investment banking roles but also surface in other job applications. If you are unsure which firms require GMAT scores, add it to your list of informational interview questions.

Competitiveness
The GMAT and GRE ranges are explicit or implicit benchmarks that the school has set to be eligible for acceptance. A proxy for the acceptance floor is the 80% range for GPA, and GMAT. Students get in with lower scores but assume that you are not one of them.

Most programs accept either exam. GMAT ranges are available for all schools, while GRE ranges are usually not published. Unless you have a legitimate reason for taking the GRE, such as pursuing a dual degree, taking the GMAT reduces future headaches and gives you a more precise benchmark for your competitiveness.

Final Notes
The military will reimburse you for taking both the GMAT and GRE (only once for each test). It does not matter which instance if you have taken either or both multiple times. For more information, check out the Defense Activity for Non-Traditional Education Support (DANTES) website. [22]

The GMAT releases all your scores from the past five years to the schools you specify, while the GRE allows you to specify which tests you want to share. Neither fact should determine which test you take. If you did not do well the first time, take the exam again. Most people

---

[22] http://www.dantes.doded.mil/examinations/funding-and-reimbursement-eligibility/reimbursement-eligibility.html#sthash.TxAUnMay.dpbs

who take the exam a second time do better (familiarity; less nervous). Having a low score and significantly improving it signals to schools that you care.

While a low score may eliminate you from consideration, a high score does not guarantee acceptance. The tests are just mandatory data points that schools and firms will use to screen candidates.

Many test-prep resources are available. Organizations such as Service to School, among others, offer veteran discounts on test prep material through partnerships with test-prep companies. A quick Google search will find the most recent offerings.

CHAPTER 6: SCHOOL-AGNOSTIC PREP

There are no secrets to success.
It is the result of preparation,
hard work, and learning from
failure. –Colin Powell

The effort you put into this part of the process will dictate your success for the next three years and beyond. You may accomplish a few more noteworthy achievements before you leave the military, but most of your stories you share will already have happened. The sooner you get started refining your stories, the better off you will be.

This section focuses on your personal brand and stories, recommenders, and résumé. Regardless of where you plan to apply, your prep here will pay dividends during your applications, business school interviews, and job interviews.

Personal Brand

Personal branding is not a new concept, but it may be new to you. Your personal brand is your reputation (in person and online). For business school applications and MBA job recruiting, having alignment between your story and your purpose is essential to land at your target school and target company. Multiple personal branding exercises are available free, but we reference the PricewaterhouseCoopers Personal Brand workbook to highlight useful takeaways. [23]

Define Your X-Factor

Your top strengths from your assessment are your X-factor. The naturally make you stand out from others. Defining your X-factor is about realizing what you are good at through self-assessment and confirming your assumptions with help from trusted people. Weave that X-factor into your essays and interview stories to convey alignment between your experiences and future goals.

Understand Your "Why" Factor

Have clear reasons why you want to accomplish the goals you have set forth. The implied task here is to ensure that your goals are not only personally meaningful, but also achievable by using what you are already great at (X-factor). Aligning your X and your Why allows the connections you make throughout the application process to be more authentic and memorable for everyone.

Eliminate Your "Zzz" Factor

This part of the exercise focuses on helping you eliminate bad habits and prepare for future networking opportunities. You need to understand the impression that you make on others and be clear on the kind of impact that you want to have. How others perceive you extends to online and off-line interactions alike.

---

[23]

https://www.pwc.com/c1/en/assets/downloads/personal_brand_workbook.pdf

Ready, Set, Show

You should now understand the gaps between how you are recognized and how you want to be perceived by others. If you are not currently where you want to be, that is OK. Awareness is the first step toward improvement. Prioritize the areas that you want to improve (i.e., public profile on LinkedIn, Twitter, personal website) and incorporate all that you have learned about yourself into a branded bio.

Your branded bio is a restatement of what makes you great (X-factor), your motivations and values (why factor), told in a compelling way (eliminate the Zzz). Send your branded bio to friends and colleagues to collect their opinions and make further edits. Once you feel comfortable, post your branded bio across all platforms where you want to have a presence (LinkedIn at a minimum).

Your Stories

You have three variety of stories that you must tell deftly:

- Accomplishments.
- Behavioral questions.
- Why questions.

Each story should follow a similar arc: explaining the situation, task, action, and result of your work (STAR). The STAR method ensures that your stories highlight your impact. If a story is not compelling after converting to the STAR format, think about the evidence you can gather to bolster you claim, or pick a different story to highlight.

Now is not the time to be deferential. Do not exaggerate your impact, but do not discount it, either. Have good reasons your accomplishments mattered to your organization, and you will be fine. When possible, align your achievements with your identified strengths. Your achievements are the evidence you will use to explain how what you did in the past applies to the role you want in the future.

Accomplishments

These are your highlights, and you should be proud of all that you have done. You should also ensure that people outside the military understand the value of your accomplishments. Remove all jargon, including acronyms, from your stories. If you are struggling, find the purpose of the acronym and use the simplified version (for example CSDP simplified is a collection of supply procedures).

Ensure that you are using data (such as percentage increase or decrease over a specified period). Lastly, ensure that you are emphasizing the "why." Why was the increase or decrease relevant to your organization? How did your action positively affect it? Now is not the time to modest. You are not doing anyone from your unit a disservice by explaining what you were able to accomplish. If you are having difficulty proving your value, try selecting different stories to highlight.

Behavioral Questions

Organizations (business schools and companies) use behavioral questions to understand what motivates you and evaluate how you solve problems. These "tell me about a time when" questions will make up much of your interviews. They can range from dealing with difficult co-workers to leading teams. Be thoughtful in your responses and think about why they are asking the questions.

For example, an interviewer asking, "Tell me about a time you failed" is asked to understand how you deal with stressful situations. Are capable of learning and growing from your mistakes? Your ability to iterate on an idea based on customer data, partner teams, and executives feedback will impact your future success. Think about the second and third order effect of your responses. What does your story communicate to your interviewer?

Why Questions

Now you get to show off your research insights. Why are you pursuing an MBA? Why do you want to work for that company? Why in the role you are seeking? Why now?

Why are you pursuing an MBA? Take it a step further and say way an MBA from that school is the missing piece between your dreams and reality (that is what they want to know). Why that firm? Because that firm operate from principles that you care about or because they have an excellent leadership development program. Asking current students their "why questions" will help you refine your own stories.

Do not mention firms that do not recruit on-campus during your essays and interviews. At best, you are indirectly minimizing the influence of the program. At worst, they will infer that you do not know the firms that hire most MBA candidates from that program.

Recommenders

Recommenders are people the school will use to validate the evidence you provide in your application. Usually, they are your past two bosses, but that does not always need to be the case. Each school has alternative options if you cannot ask your current boss.

If you just went through the effort to compile your stories, this part is simple. Share your branded bio and your relevant stories with your potential recommenders. You usually need two recommenders for each school. There are two options:

Straightforward: Choose your last two bosses.

Work backward: Do you know what kind of experiences the school values? Is your supervisor a graduate of one of your target schools? Are you applying to a lot of different programs?

Using more than two recommenders reduces the effort it takes for them to help you (See Figure 6-1 below). Recommendations are opportunities to reinforce your stated goals (essays) and fill gaps in your candidacy. For example, if you did not get a high quant score on the GMAT, but your recommender describes a time you made a data-driven decision that helped the organization, it can help ease concerns about your quantitative abilities.

Schools	First Recommender	Second Recommender
1 School 1	Joe	Jim
2 School 2	Joe	Dave
3 School 3	Jim	Dave

Figure 6-1. Example MBA recommender template.

Recommender Packet[24]

Regardless of your chosen approach, you need to put together a packet for each recommender. In this packet you should:

- Highlight your accomplishments while you worked together.
- Explain your motivations for getting an MBA.
- Include the essay questions from each school and define what each school is looking for from prospective candidates.
- Give clear submission instructions and deadlines.

I advise giving your recommenders eight weeks before the deadline to complete your recommendation. You know their bandwidth, output rate and field training schedule best, so adjust to your comfort level.

---

[24] Recommender packet template found on website under the Resources tab.

You want to avoid a circumstance where a missing recommendation prevents you from submitting your application. After you are through the admissions process, do not forget to thank them for their help and let them know which school you choose. Even if it is not the school they helped you with, they will want to hear how you did and offer their congratulations.

Résumé

We are not going to go too deep into résumé format. Regardless of the format you choose now, you will need to adjust it to your school once you are accepted. Multiple acceptable MBA résumé formats are online. You can usually find a template for your target school online or ask for a copy of a résumé when you are do student informational interviews. Format aside, there are a few rules you should follow:

Highlights

Maintain a separate document from your résumé to list all your accomplishment bullets, allowing you to customize the résumé as necessary for each job application. Keep your bullets accomplishment-oriented. Your résumé is not a place to list your responsibilities, so ditch the "responsible for X of personnel and $X of equipment" bullet. Start by tying your accomplishments to the awards you received. Your awards are the results of your actions. Now, pull your highlights from your evaluations. Use percentages, ratios, and rankings to demonstrate your impact.

Structure

Keep it to one page. The basic structure of your résumé bullets should look like (all in the past tense) "you did X, because of Y, which resulted in Z." An alternative is "because of Y, you did X, which resulted in Z." The "Z" needs to be impactful and jargon-free. Vary your first verb (the thesaurus in your friend). Each bullet needs to be two lines or less, with the most impactful bullet first.

CHAPTER 7: SCHOOL-SPECIFIC APPLICATIONS

Great spirits have always
encountered violent opposition
from mediocre minds.
—Albert Einstein

This is where the rubber meets the road! It is time to compile all your efforts and persuade your target school to accept you. You should focus your efforts on the schools you genuinely want to attend. Use your quantitative and qualitative assessments to choose programs that best fit your situation and goals.

If there are programs you are excited about, but you do not meet their published 80% ranges, do not be afraid to apply to those "reach" schools. You will sleep better at night after receiving a rejection letter from a reach school than wondering "what if?" years later. You never know what is in the mind of the admissions officer reviewing your packet, and your story may be compelling enough to overlook any weak points in your application. This next section covers:

- When to apply.
- How to approach writing your essays.
- How to prepare for admissions interviews.

When to Apply

The best time to apply is once you have your most robust profile (GMAT, GPA, work accomplishments) ready to share. The earlier your profile is ready, the less stressful the rest of your application process will be. Some schools also give admissions and scholarship preference to candidates who apply during an "early decision" period, so being ready early allows you to take advantage of the opportunity.

If you are not committed to an "early decision" application, you need to reach out to the veterans' club at your target school. They will let you know about and invite you to their prospective student, veteran-specific programming. Attending one (or more) of these events will ensure that the admissions committee knows who you are when they review your application.

When scheduling a school visit, sign up for coffee chats with current students, attend a class, and go on a campus tour. The personalization you will be able to infuse into your essays will be invaluable. In short, if you are planning to visit campus, do not apply until after your visit (veteran programming or not).

Application Prioritization

I recommend applying to the schools you want to attend the most first (early decision, round one, and round two). Doing so aligns your incentives and eliminates the need send a deposit to a school you may not attend. You want to put the maximum amount of effort into your target schools, so do not apply to your safety school at the same time. It is difficult to be excited about more than a few programs at a time.

Here is an example scenario. You spend all your effort applying to a top 10 school in round one and get waitlisted. In round two you retake the GMAT, get a better score, and share that with your round one school. In round three, you spend all your effort applying to a top 30 school and get accepted. Prior to sending in your acceptance to your top 30 school, your round one school contacts you to let you know you have been accepted off their waitlist. Had you applied to both schools in round one, and not given maximum effort to your target school in the beginning, you may have gotten dinged (denied acceptance) as opposed to waitlisted.

Essays

Your pre-MBA stories will be the primary points of differentiation from other candidates (that you can control). Your experiences were different from those of most candidates, so use that novelty to your advantage. Look back at the moments that made you think business school was the right choice for you and weave them into your story.

During your informational interviews, you should probe for what principles and values your essays need to highlight. Our focus here is on universal tips.

Answer the Essay Question you are Asked, not the one you Want to Answer.

You have a personal narrative that tells people "Why business school?" You need your narrative, but it may not be what they are asking for, or not in the same format you are used to sharing. Ensure that the structure of your essay answers their fundamental questions.

For example, if you are asked to provide your short-term goals, long-term goals, and reasons for wanting to get an MBA, answer those questions, in that order. Do not spend so much time with your intro that you skimp on your immediate next steps post-MBA. As you get further out (long-term goals), you can be less concrete, but the progression needs to be natural and logical.

Create an outline for each essay prompt to provide structure to your story. Think about what information you are already sharing with the admissions committee in other parts of your application. Do not be a broken record, and do not recycle entire essays from one school application to another. Make sure you are highlighting the reasons why their MBA program would unlock your goals. Each essay needs to be personalized, or else you will come off as generic.

Be Authentic

Focus on be the most authentic version of yourself. Tell a story that only you can tell. Make it personal, be vulnerable and do your best to evoke emotion from the reader. If your essay elicits an emotional response from the reader, you are on the right track.

Trusted Parties

If you have friends and family who never have constructive things to say, chances are they are not your target audience. You want people who know you well enough to determine if your essays seem authentic. They also need to be comfortable giving you feedback when your story does not flow well, does not answer the question or over-emphasizes a trivial point. Having a thick skin and giving yourself enough time to create multiple drafts of each essay will go a long way in producing a stellar set of essays.

If you do not have people you can rely on for this type of feedback, an admissions consultant can be helpful. There are many paid and unpaid admissions consultants who will be willing to look at (not write) your essays and provide feedback. Evaluate paid admission consultants from their online reviews, do a free consultation and understand ahead of time that your mileage may vary.

Admissions Interview Prep

Dress Code

Dress to impress. You need to look well put together. Spend the money to have your interview outfit tailored. Depending on your body type, the difference between off the rack and tailored clothing can be enormous. You will look better, feel better and have a better interview. For men, suit and tie are appropriate. For women, I recommend conservative business attire (with jacket). If you are uncertain about school-specific formalities, ask about dress codes during your first few informational interviews.

Interview Questions

The internet is your best resource for up-to-date, school-specific interview tactics. There are multiple websites and blogs to help you. If you are looking to bolster your research, incorporate questions around the admissions interview process into your TIARA framework (Insights and Advice) when speaking with current students. You will notice trends and can then plan accordingly.

At a minimum, you need to have your behavioral stories and "Why" questions down pat. They do not have to be lengthy responses. To avoid detail overload for your interviewer, keep your answers to 30 to 60 seconds and follow the STAR format discussed in Chapter 6. Shorter responses allow the interview to feel more like a conversation and less like an interrogation. You want to come off as thoughtful but not scripted.

Before you arrive, scan the internet for recent articles published about the school, check in with the veterans' club to see if you can meet someone before or after, and relax. The day of the interview, listen to something funny, call an old friend, or meditate. Whatever helps you relax, do it.

Expect to have a curveball or two thrown your way. Mine was, "What if all of your recruiting efforts fall through, what's your backup plan?". In hindsight, it was an easy question, but I was surprised at the time. Do your best to roll with any surprises and make sure you have questions for the admissions officer or student who is conducting your interview. Pull a few insight and advice type questions from your TIARA question bank or ask about a recent initiative at school or in the city.

If all goes well, you will hear back from your target school in a few weeks and have a difficult (but enviable) decision to make. Take time to discuss it with your family and friends, talk to more people at your target school if needed and go to the admit weekend if you can to meet your (potential) new classmates.

If things did not go well, decide if you have other schools you want to apply for this year, or if you're going to wait a year and try the process again. There is no shame in reapplying next year, and schools look favorably toward re-applicants if they have strengthened their profiles from the previous year.

PART III: CONVINCE TARGET COMPANIES

Maximizing Your Finite Resources

CHAPTER 8: THE VOID

From acceptance letters to MBA orientation

We think by feeling. What is
there to know?
—Theodore Roethke

Due diligence complete! If you have only one offer, you must decide if that program will help you achieve your aspirations. If everything aligns, graciously accept. If you are not jumping at the opportunity to attend, do not go. You can earn only one MBA.

If you have multiple offers, it is time to take a more qualitative approach. What is your gut saying? Still unconvinced? Here are a few considerations to help you decide.

Final Steps

This is the first time during the application process when you have all the leverage. Enjoy the brief reprieve and use these four areas to be clear about which school is right for you.

Admit Weekends

Each program hosts an "admitted students" weekend. These weekends include aspirational programming by top professors and student clubs. These events present a glamorized "day-in-the-life" of an MBA student, with networking, cocktails and fancy meals. This event is about assessing "fit". Fit can encompass several aspects, but you should focus on:

- **Culture**: Is the vibe collaborative or cut-throat? Competition elevates, but divisiveness can make the academic/recruiting process less productive.
- **Chemistry**: Do you get along well with your potential classmates? Would you spend time with them outside school? Think about the lifelong network.
- **Competency**: Do you feel like the smartest person in the room? Are you surrounding yourself with other high-achieving students and professors who will push you to do your best work? Will you be challenged and grow there?

There will be students who have already sent in their deposits and prospective students who are still on the fence. If you are undecided, use this opportunity to seek out the committed students. Ask them what made the difference for them and consider their points against your concerns. You should have a solid idea if you fit in after the weekend.

Offers and Scholarships
If you are juggling offers with varying levels of financial support, it is in your best interest to tell the smaller-offer school. Reach out to the person who communicated your acceptance, or your primary point of contact in the admissions office (veteran admissions officer). Explain how you enjoyed your interactions during the recruiting process, admit weekend, or any other programming they hosted, but that the financial incentives from the other schools are giving you pause on deciding. Is there anything they can do to make the decision more straightforward for you (match the offer)?

It helps if the programs offering you more money are close with your top choice in the MBA rankings. Do not expect a top-five school to match the financial aid package from a program in the mid-40s. Also, do not expect an immediate decision. Give them enough time to decide, and if they come back with concessions, excellent! If they do not increase your financial aid, thank them for reviewing it and do not bring it up again.

Remember, financial considerations should not be the primary driver of your decision. You are getting an MBA for the long-term payoff. If your top choice does not give you the most money, it still might the best program for you.

Deposits
If you still cannot decide, you can always send deposits to the schools that gave you offers. You should have a visceral feeling when sending those deposits (generally a few thousand dollars for each school). Listen to those feelings. If it feels wrong as you go to hit the submit deposit button, do not do it!

10-10-10 Rule
Suzy Welch, in her book "10-10-10", recommends a three-pronged framework for decision-making. [25]

- How will you feel about the decision you are contemplating in 10 minutes?
- How will you feel about it in 10 months?
- How will you feel about it in 10 years?

---

[25] 10-10-10: 10 Minutes, 10 Months, 10 Years - A Life-Transforming Idea by Suzy Welch

We tend to agonize over our present-day decisions. Framing the decision with a long-term view will help surface your true feelings for which school is right for you. I used this advice for my internship decision (Amazon versus Google versus Bridgewater versus American Express), and in my personal life. If the framework is good enough for Warren Buffet and Ray Dalio, it is sage advice for you. [26]

Realistically, you must set a hard deadline for deciding (generally when fall tuition is due, but it could be earlier due to your final Permanent Change of Station timeline). If you have more than one offer from schools that give you similar opportunities post-graduation, it is impossible for you to make a bad choice. Be honest with yourself about your motivations for business school, choose a school and be thankful for the opportunities ahead of you.

Pre-MBA Internships

Your transition timeline will dictate if a pre-MBA internship is possible. If you are getting out and have more than a few months before school starts, a pre-MBA internship can be tremendously helpful once fall recruiting begins. Some pre-MBA opportunities are veteran-specific, but not all of them. Also, not all internships are "pre-MBA internships." Review the best industry-specific internships first, not just the veteran and MBA opportunities.

A pre-MBA internship is the lowest risk way to tell if you want to work in an industry. Is it interesting? Do you enjoy your co-workers? Is your future school held in high regard? These are signals you should use to inform your recruiting strategy. Do an outstanding job, as you would in any undertaking, and quantify your impact with your supervisor.

---

[26] http://www.businessinsider.com/i-tried-the-101010-method-inspired-by-warren-buffett-and-ray-dalio-2017-10

Afterward, you will have to decide whether the experience is worth putting on your résumé. If it was a valuable experience and you intend to be recruited in the same industry, it will be immensely helpful. If you decide you want to work in a different industry, including the internship on your résumé will be less valuable. However, if you have just saved yourself by rejecting a career you would not have enjoyed, bravo! Work with your career services office for more specific guidance on what to include on your résumé for summer internship recruiting.

Paid and Unpaid Internships

It is ideal to land an internship that is in your target industry and will pay you. If they are paying, they will give you more responsibility. However, many internships are unpaid. The paid versus unpaid conundrum is industry-specific and does not indicate your usefulness. Remember why you are looking for an internship in the first place. Short-term monetary gain is not your motivation. Unpaid internships can lead to paid internships and full-time roles, so do not discount them.

Veteran Workshops and Summits

The most accessible opportunities for veterans are multi-day workshops or summits. Firms that are looking to hire veterans will host these events to give insight into the types of experiences and training they value (expect employers in the same industry to have similar viewpoints). These events will also put you on their recruiting radar. These events always require applications, so check the deadlines to make sure you do not miss a one-time opportunity.

Diversity Recruiting

Veterans are diversity candidates for firms. Diversity consideration is a double-edged sword. The positive aspect is that you have a realistic opportunity to work for most firms that recruit MBAs. A potential downside is that many firms have preconceived notions about the type of work you will be good at and may not be willing to put you in a role in which you do not have experience.

If you want to stay in a similar career field, staying in a similar-function role makes sense. There is benefit (to a firm and to you) in hitting the ground running. It puts you in the position to immediately demonstrate your value and confirms to that firm that you are worth additional investment if you want to change roles later. I recruited with Google to work on its Finance Operations team (I was in finance roles in my last few positions in the Army), but I wanted to become a product manager (which I could not do at Google without a technical background). The realization that I could not be a PM at Google led me to look at opportunities with other firms.

It is your responsibility to connect the dots for your future employers and make it clear why you are a good fit for a new role. If you are looking to switch functions as well (for example, HR to marketing, finance to product management, operations to consulting), figuring out which firms would allow you to branch out beyond your experience is a large part of the recruiting process.

If you attend a veteran MBA career fair before school, be wary. You are in the information-gathering stage, not the commitment stage. Many firms at these career fairs will accept applications for summer internships and might even offer to interview you at the career fair. That sounds great, right? Not exactly. The purpose of these early interviews is to ensure that diversity candidates get a fair chance in recruiting. However, you are not ready to present your best self to future employers.

Recruiters have a set of criteria they use to evaluate potential hires. Their requirements do not change for veterans and do not change because you are recruiting three to six months before other potential hires.

Remember why you decided to get an MBA. *You want to increase the probability that you land your dream job.* The purpose of the MBA was not so you can drop a few hundred thousand dollars to gain access to a career fair. You still need to spend time crafting your narrative, building connections through your alumni base and leveraging your career services office before sitting down to interview with firms.

One helpful approach in this low-pressure situation (it is low pressure because you have already decided that you will not be interviewing today) is to ask the employers what they are looking for in their candidates (not just their veteran candidates). You should take those traits and find stories in your past to show those competencies. If you cannot reach a recruiter during the career fair, use the job descriptions as a signal for the traits they value. For example, recruiters look for candidates with the ability to work and deliver results in uncertain environments. Find the best story that shows your ability to thrive in ambiguous circumstances and ask recruiters their opinions. If you use their feedback to strengthen your story, you will stand out when interviews come around.

Enjoy the early exposure, refine your story, and network with other motivated veterans you will undoubtedly run into again on the recruiting trail.

CHAPTER 9: PRE-INTERNSHIP OFFER

Year 1: First semester

"All progress takes place outside
the comfort zone."
—Michael John Bobak

Congratulations, you did it!

Now prepare to be uncomfortable again. Your first semester will provide multiple opportunities to show off the "highly functional in an uncertain environment" skills you cultivated in the military. Do not fret. Everyone else is as unsure of their future as you are. If you are not nervous, you are not pushing yourself enough and are missing a once-in-a-lifetime opportunity to grow.

This chapter is broken into four sections focusing on time allocation, information gathering, points of differentiation and getting involved.

Time Allocation

Proper time allocation is the first step in creating the conditions for a successful first semester. In the military, we recommend a two-thirds planning and one-third execution timeframe. Business school also has an ideal timeframe breakdown: one-third each for coursework, recruiting and clubs.

Coursework

First-semester coursework consists of core classes in subjects all MBAs are expected to be proficient in, such as accounting, statistics and strategy. Your familiarity with the core coursework will dictate how much time you need to spend on these subjects.

Now is an excellent time to review your school's grade-disclosure policy. If your grades are disclosed during recruiting, they will be used to differentiate you from other candidates but grades are not a primary focus (for employers or for yourself). If your school practices grade nondisclosure, that applies only to on-campus recruiting. If you recruit off-campus, your grades are fair game.

Most of your courses will have group projects and use on a forced curve. You need to learn these subjects but understand that you are not going to receive an internship offer from what you learn in the first semester of business school (even with a 4.0). Business fundamentals are table stakes, not differentiators.

Recruiting

Unless you have experience in recruiting for high-paying jobs, expect the recruiting process to be a high-effort activity. Your ability to sell yourself to others will have a direct impact on your future job prospects. Each school will have a different method, but at a minimum expect to have your:

- 30 second-pitch.
- 60 second-pitch.
- Résumé highlighting your accomplishments (not your responsibilities).

You need to be able to explain, in person, why you are interested in a role, company, or industry. You will have multiple instances to tell your story during your one-on-one and group networking sessions. Understand the context of your situation (know your audience) and remove all jargon from your stories. You should be able to explain your pitch to someone without any military experience. Think about what you tell your family and friends during holidays or social gatherings. If your grandmother gives you a quizzical look when you explain why your experience lends itself to a career in finance, your story needs modifying. If you are struggling with this, reach out to your career-services office to schedule a one-on-one coaching session before on-campus recruiting starts in late September or October (school specific).

At the beginning of the semester, plot your target companies on a networking effort versus impact chart (Figure 9-1 below). Determine which firms are high-touch (networking is required to get an interview) and which are low-touch (résumé drops; networking is for information-gathering only and does not impact recruiting). MBA2s and your career-services office will help you decide where each company lies if you cannot figure it out for yourself. Do you best to avoid high-effort, low-efficacy recruiting (like case competitions for companies where you are not actively recruiting). Do you enjoy the activities involved to recruit with these firms? High-touch firms deal with clients regularly, while low-touch firms are further from customers (not in impact but in day-to-day interactions).

Figure 9-1. Recruiting effort chart for all target companies.

Professional Clubs

Clubs provide a safe opportunity to engage with students, professors, and alumni focused on the same industries and opportunities. If you are a career-switcher and want to show initiative to your future employer, volunteer to be on a club board. For example, if you are interested in consulting, join the management consulting club and become a member of that board, responsible for a bringing in speakers to address the club (equivalent to an additional duty, but with more benefits). It may not land you a job directly, but you will benefit from the industry immersion.

FOMO

At some point, you are going to suffer from the fear of missing out (FOMO). Multiple extracurricular events, target company sessions and industry training opportunities will overlap. Stay focused and remember what your initial motivation for business school was in the first place. It is OK if your career goals have changed since you started school, as long as your time allocation reflects your change in focus.

Information Gathering

At the heart of your personal and professional growth, your goal is to land a job that you will enjoy and allows you to be great. To do that, you need to engage with people at your target companies. Below is a spectrum of people familiar with your target companies and who are willing to help you (highest likelihood to least likely).

MBA2s

MBA2s should be your first stop, as they were in your shoes just a year ago. You will find most MBA2s willing to help you, and they will give you unfiltered perspective on what it is like to work at your target company.

If you can find out, focus your initial efforts on MBA2s who received offers to return to your target company. This approach reduces the awkwardness of asking someone to relive a negative experience (not receiving an offer to return). To maximize the benefit of informational interviews, follow a structured process such as Steve Dalton's TIARA (Trends, Insights, Advice, Resources, Assignments) from Chapter 3.

Military Veterans at Your Target Company
Military veterans at your target company should be your next step in information interview phase. Use LinkedIn to find these people if you are not already in contact with the firm. Veteran alumni from your school are the best resource (check with your military veterans' club for an alumni database), but often the shared military service connection will be enough to get on any military veteran's calendar. If you are still formulating your pitch for why your transition from the military is a good fit for a role at your target company (always tailor your message to your audience), this is an opportunity to see if your approach will resonate.

The conversation should not explicitly center on your shared past. Follow your established TIARA framework and remember that the main benefits of this touchpoint are:

- An unfiltered viewpoint on what it is like to work there.
- Insight into the company's diversity hiring pipeline.

Always be professional and remember that the person you are speaking to may impact whether you get an interview. Unless you know the person well (outside of this interaction) do not ask for a personal referral. Most companies limit personal referrals, and a reference before you are ready to put your best foot forward will put you at a disadvantage against other applicants. [27]

Alumni at Your Target Company
This group should include your undergraduate and graduate networks. The effectiveness of this approach will depend on your method of connection (alumni databases, LinkedIn or in-person) and availability. Expect response rates to be lower than from the veterans

---

[27] https://leap.ai/blog/2017/10/19/power_of_quality_referrals

in industry and your school's MBA2s and give them ample time to respond. Do not email them three days before your first interview and expect a response. Remember to ask questions specific to their roles and keep in mind that the hiring process is always changing.

Your goal is to be as prepared as possible when your target company comes to campus for corporate presentations, diversity recruiting events or invitation-only events at its office. The insights you gain will make your networking conversations more impactful and allow you to write a cover letter that will stand out.

Corporate Presentations

Companies that recruit on campus start by hosting an on-campus presentation. Alumni employees from your program (or HR) run these events. Structurally, the presentations give an overview of the company, available roles for the summer and an opportunity to ask questions. There is usually time to mingle at the end for questions you do not want to ask publicly. These events are great ways to connect with alumni at your target company. Nearly all companies take attendance, and certain companies use attendance as a screening criterion. Unless you have an internal referral, you need to attend the corporate presentation. If you are in a bind from multiple commitments, reach out to MBA2s and ask if attendance is mandatory. Your actions are signals to the firm of how much you want to work there. Do not give them a reason to cut you as a candidate before you get a chance to interview.

Treks

Treks are office visits and tours of your target company. If you are in a larger city, these opportunities will be more abundant throughout the school year. For schools in more remote locations, treks to larger cities are commonplace during school breaks. View these trips as another opportunity to learn about and evaluate a company. If the trek is made before your interview (or if you interview while you are on the trek), feel free to discuss the trip as another reason you know you want to work there.

Once you have a summer internship offer from a firm, you will find that your alumni at that firm will be more willing to meet with you and recommend how to be successful over the summer. Use these opportunities to learn more about your future company.

Points of Differentiation

To stand out, you need to invest in efforts that will differentiate you from other candidates. Refer to your touch versus effort matrix. What signals of fit can you send to your target company that others may overlook or not take advantage of?

Case Competitions

One often-overlooked way to stand out is to participate in school-affiliated or national case competitions. Each competition will have a different timeframe, resource commitment and payout. Even if you are not successful (bounced after the first round), the research that you put into your case will pay dividends. If you are selected to compete in multiple rounds, you will understand the motivations of your target company even better. These competitions usually have the added benefit of cash prizes and may get you an interview.

Applications

Each organization has a different application-intake process, ranging from cover letters, essays, and interactive assessments to pure résumé drops. Use the application as another signal of what is important to the company. As a rule of thumb, applications with minimal touchpoints (résumé drop only, no cover letter), will be screened for keywords before recruiters look at them. Review their job postings to ensure that the language you are using in your application matches theirs. Keywords that show up in the job postings you will apply for (or a close substitute) should find their way into your résumé and cover letters.

Cover Letters

A cover letter is a document that you send with your résumé to explain to companies why you are a good fit for the role you are applying to. Will they be the bane of your existence? Maybe, but take this opportunity to set yourself apart from other applicants. Most schools have a generic cover letter template to follow. Do not send the template without making the cover letter personal.

Use the cover letter to demonstrate your knowledge of the company, and focus on their needs, not yours. [28] Try to understand why the company is hiring for the position. Do not spend time explaining your previous accomplishments, but rather focus on what you would bring to the role. Give an example of a recommended improvement in the company that you would be able to influence in your desired role. Ask others during your informational interviews for an improvement they would like to see if you cannot think of one.

Get Involved

Most of this semester is about tapping new resources and gleaning the insights of others. Joining clubs will help prepare you for your internship. Clubs function as aggregators of information and opportunities. As a career-switcher, (most student veterans), integrating into your target industry has to happen as soon as possible.

---

[28] https://medium.com/brightcrowd/make-an-offer-they-cant-refuse-a7f2d22d3787

Professional Clubs
Professional clubs (such as consulting, investment banking, technology, and entrepreneurship) are gateways to build your domain knowledge within your desired industry. Expect programming to come from current students, alumni and companies that want to recruit members from each club. Professional clubs are also responsible for annual industry conferences and for organizing treks to individual companies. A fantastic way to signal to a firm that you are interested in it is to join the industry's club board (for example, McKinsey aligns with the management consulting club).

Affinity Clubs
Affinity clubs (veterans, gender, ethnicity and sexual orientation, for example) are great at building community. Many things are changing for you in the first semester and having a level of continuity and fellowship is important. Affinity clubs also host speakers on campus and have access to diversity hiring events.

Prospective Student Support
During your recruiting and coursework, expect to field multiple requests for coffee chats from prospective students. People from your network who are applying to business school will also reach out. During orientation, the administration will also ask for volunteers to connect with prospective students.

Think back to where you were just a year ago, and how the benevolence of current students made a difference as you decided where you wanted to spend your next two years. You will find these interactions rewarding as you help shepherd the next class of students forward in their careers.

CHAPTER 10: POST-INTERNSHIP OFFER

Year 1: Second semester

Some people dream of success,
while other people get up every
morning and make it happen
—Wayne Huizenga

You are either basking in short-lived glory or still hunting for your ideal internship. If you have your summer internship offer in hand, congratulations! If you are still looking for your summer internship, that is fine, too. Each industry has a different recruiting timeline and companies within an industry vary from established recruiting cycles for larger firms to just-in-time hiring for smaller firms. Regardless of your situation, your direction is forward. Use your time to you maximize your potential for success.

We break this chapter into three sections: time allocation, coursework/skill building and club leadership roles.

Time Allocation

Your second semester will be more enjoyable. With the newness of business school wearing off, your understanding of how to be successful will increase your efficiency. How you spend your time will depend on your internship status. Here are baseline recommendations. Adjust to fit your situation and comfort level.

Offer in hand

If you already have your offer, you should do a 50/50 split between coursework/skill building and club/extracurricular activities. The second semester is your first opportunity to own your schedule. Build in downtime and do not forget self-care (like the gym and meditation). You do not want to burn out before the summer starts.

Active Recruiting

Recruiting takes priority here, with a 50/30/20 split between recruiting, coursework, and club activities. When forming groups for project-based assignments, ensure that you have a few members who have finished recruiting. You do not want everyone in your team devoting all their time to recruiting or your projects will suffer. Everyone understands that getting hired is your main priority and they will help you pick up the slack if you ask and are transparent. Work with your career office to refine your recruiting plan. Often the career office will know how to engage with companies that practice just-in-time hiring (on and off campus) and can help position you for those opportunities.

If you have already interviewed and your interviews did not go well, be honest with yourself. Did you spread yourself to thin? Did your time allocation match your desired goals? Self-reflection, your classmates and the careers office will help you land your summer internship before the semester ends.

Coursework and Skill Building

You are either locked into a required curriculum for the first year or taking elective curriculum. Reach out to MBA2s who are going back to your target company. What classes and opportunities did they take advantage of that helped them most in their internships?

Required Curriculum

With required curriculum, look for clubs, partner schools, organizations, workshops and other events in your area. Applying for a spring internship is another way to build (or confirm) your business skills for future employers.

Elective Curriculum

For students with elective curriculum, take a mix of coursework that is interesting, has the best-rated professors and is useful for your summer internship. The best professors have wisdom that will end up affecting your internship or life in ways you cannot predict from reading the syllabus or word of mouth. Skill building is more straightforward for elective curriculum. Take a course in modeling financial statements if you will have to build financial models during your internship. Enroll in a data-mining class if you have to draw insights from large data sets. Not all your classes need to be focused on the internship, but adding one or two will help you hit the ground running.

Your required curriculum will ensure that you can meet the expectations of your employers over the summer. Use your elective curriculum or external opportunities to bring skills and thought processes to your internship that are nontraditional but complementary.

For example, I took an elective course called Tech Product Management. Going into a role in product management, I considered it a required course. I learned how to generate digital sketches of my product ideas to generate discussion using the user interface design tool Balsamiq. I used Balsamiq in my internship with remarkable success to work with the design team to introduce new features. I also took a data-mining course. I learned how to apply machine learning models to solve problems like when to target a customer for a promotion and how to figure out which customer attributes matter most. I used insights from that class to recommend product improvements to my summer project. The combination of those two was a big reason I was offered a full-time position later.

Generating new insights for your firm will bring you one step closer to securing a full-time offer.

Club Leadership Roles

You know what clubs added value to your first semester. Do you want to be involved in those clubs in your second year? If so, you should strongly consider running for the board or president. If you are going to be involved, you might as well help run the organization. If you are actively recruiting, you should look for a lower-effort role or a co-president to help you (most presidents are co-presidents). Limit your board involvement to two positions, unless you know you will have a lot of free time during the second year.

You are coming into business school with more direct leadership experience than your peers. View this as another opportunity for you to give back to your school and deepen your understanding of an industry or affinity group. It boils down to leaving an organization better than you found it, and we are all capable of doing that. How are you going to help ensure the future success of your school?

CHAPTER 11: GOING BACK TO TARGET COMPANY

Year 2

What you get by achieving your goals is not as important as what you become by achieving your goals.
—Zig Ziglar

Well done! The goal you set when you began thinking about your transition is nearly complete! You have an offer to return post-graduation, and you have a few decisions to make, including whether to accept the offer. The fact you own the decision whether to return is empowering, and your self-confidence should be at an all-time high. This chapter focuses on what to do if you are accepting your offer and Chapter 12 will cover the steps if you decide to reject your offer and re-recruit.

This chapter has five sections: time allocation, coursework/skill building, recruiting within your firm, club initiatives and helping others.

Time Allocation

Take a moment to reflect on the part of business school to which you want to devote more time. A 25/25/25/25 split between coursework, return-firm recruiting, clubs and helping others is an excellent starting point.

Coursework and Skill Building

It can be challenging to stay motivated by coursework when you know you have a job already lined up but do your best to maintain your focus.

You should have a clear grasp of the knowledge and skill gaps between where you are and where you need to be before starting your full-time role. A helpful approach is to take more soft-skill classes in the fall and leave your hard-skill courses for the spring. Ordering your courses in this manner ensures that your hard skills are still fresh in your mind when you start your job. Check the availability of the professors you still want to have and see when they teach, slotting their courses into your plan.

Your last year of business school is also the last time you will have so much flexibility in your schedule. Front-load or back-load your classes to give yourself a built-in 4-day weekend if you want. If you are not a morning person, take afternoon and evening classes. The level of freedom you have right now is unrivaled. Enjoy it!

In-firm Recruiting

During the summer you meaningfully expanded your in-firm network. Some companies emphasize this practice more than others, but most companies provide flexible placement for interns returning full-time. With the pressure of the internship over, reconnect with your contacts. If you had particularly engaging conversations, follow up with them. If you are interested in their team, ask if that team is hiring.

The informational interview guides that you used over the past few years will be less helpful in figuring out where to work within an organization. There are online resources to help. The Breakout List, found on Medium and Twitter, has a guide to interviewing your future manager, which you should adapt to your needs.[29] These types of questions include but are not limited to:

- Why did you join the firm?
- What is one thing that makes you think the firm is doing really well?
- How are projects managed and reported (such as RACI or ad hoc)? [30]

Use every opportunity you can to vet your future manager and team. The best managers will welcome your questions and give concise answers. If you are getting the runaround, be wary. We have all experienced the benefits of an incredible manager and the downside of a poor manager. You finally have some influence on who your manager is; do not let it go to waste.

Club Initiatives

Do you remember where you were just a year ago? If you are running a club or are a vice president of a club, expect to receive a lot of requests from first-year and prospective students. Help where you can and be sure to invest the right amount of time in each of your club commitments. The impact you have as a vice president or president

---

[29] https://notes.breakoutlist.com/guide-to-interviewing-your-future-manager-before-deciding-where-to-work-3b2eb3326793
[30] RACI- Responsible, Accountable, Consulted, Informed

ripples throughout the school and leaves a lasting impression on current and prospective students.

Helping Others

First-year students look for guidance on how to approach recruiting and how to position themselves to get an offer at your firm. Prospective students are looking for the same connections you were to make one of the most influential decisions of their lives. Be as generous as you can with your time without losing your sanity. Blocking time on your calendar is the easiest way to balance these requests. When you receive thank-you emails letting you know about offers they got from your firm or acceptance to your school, you will know that your time was well spent.

CHAPTER 12: RE-RECRUITING

Year 2

Challenges are what make life interesting and overcoming them is what makes life meaningful.
—Joshua J. Marine

You are in one of two camps right now. Either you have an offer in hand but are trying to use it to leverage a better offer (different firm, same industry or same firm, different role) before your initial offer expires, or you did not receive an offer to return from your summer internship and are recruiting out of necessity. Re-recruiting after an offer is made follows a similar path to returning to a full-time role with the same company (Chapter 11). We will outline a few best practices to consider, but most of this chapter focuses on re-recruiting out of necessity.

Time Allocation for Optional Re-recruiting

A good place to start is a 25/25/25/25 split between re-recruiting, coursework, clubs and helping others.

Re-Recruiting on Your Own Accord

There are a few questions you should ask yourself before you start re-recruiting.

What is Your Motivation for re-recruiting?

- Better esteem in the market?
- More enjoyable work?
- Better career trajectory?
- Better skill-development opportunities?
- Better location?
- Better pay/benefits?

Having clarity on these questions before you begin applying and interviewing will help you make a better decision. Be clear to yourself about what criteria are negotiable and which are not (for you and your target firms).

Is the Role you are Recruiting for Held in the Same Esteem as Your Summer Position?

Each company will have one part that has the most influence. For example, if you join a financial services firm, marketing roles have a more significant impact than product management roles. In a tech firm, product management roles are more impactful and marketing has less influence. Each firm has a different dynamic, and it is helpful to understand where you will fit in the organization's decision-making hierarchy before you accept a role.

Once you begin interviewing, pay attention to how other firms in the market see your summer firm. If your interviewers spend most of the interview fawning over your summer company, the interviewing firm is probably not where you want to end up.

We break down the rest of this chapter into time allocation, setting expectations, tapping your network, coursework/skill building, and helping others.

Time Allocation for Required Re-recruiting

The most important thing from the start of your second year until you graduate is landing your post-MBA job. If your dream job is still out there, go for it! If not, think about taking a role that will allow you to transition into your ideal position in 18 to 24 months after graduation. Until you have a full-time offer, a 50/25/25 split between re-recruiting, coursework and helping others is perfect. Once you have a full-time offer in hand, feel free to allocate more of your time to your coursework and extracurricular activities.

Setting Expectations

One thing we know for sure, you are not going back to your previous company. Now that that is out of the way, what is next?

Just like every other job you have had in the past, there were positives and negatives. What did you learn about the company, yourself, and your target industry? Be honest with yourself about why you are not going back. Was it that the company that was not a great fit, or the role? Focus on the positive aspects of your internship. You are going to need to tell those stories throughout your upcoming interviews.

There is an unseen benefit to re-recruiting in your second year. You are more polished and focused. Also, full-time hiring is less complicated. Recruiting firms have a role to fill, and you want to fill that role. The developmental opportunities that an internship program affords are not guaranteed, but you can still land a position that allows you to develop while harnessing your strengths.

Tapping Your Network

Now is not the time to be bashful. You have spent the past year building your network, deliberately or not. Once you have your target-company list, review LinkedIn and your available alumni databases. First-degree connections are always preferred, but second and third-degree connections are better than no connection at all. Ask to be introduced to friends of friends and alumni who work or interned at your target firms.

Your careers office is also motivated to help you get a job. Scrape the internal job boards daily. Meet with a career coach to go over your self-assessment and target company list. Stay composed. You will have clarity soon.

Club Initiatives

Your ability to help with club initiatives will be limited while you are recruiting again. If you are in a leadership position, be clear about your availability with your club. Even if you cannot be as involved as you expected when you took the role, you can still be helpful. By setting clear expectations for your first-year board members, you will be going a long way toward ensuring the club's success.

Helping Others

First-year students are looking for guidance on how to approach recruiting and how to position themselves to get an offer at your summer firm. You are not returning, but you can still provide a meaningful perspective to first-year students who are working through their options.

EPILOGUE: PAY IT FORWARD

You now own the framework for making the most of your MBA experience. Regardless of where you are in the process, I hope this book has added value.

It is never too early to lend a hand. If you have friends or colleagues who are thinking about getting their MBAs, share the resources you have found along the way.

Once you get into school, think about the best ways to help other veterans at your school, in your network, or outside of your network. Many veteran nonprofits (and nonprofits in general) would love to tap into your expertise. You will find that your skills from the military are still valuable. You just need to explain them in a way that others can understand.

The positive impact you will have on your classmates and prospective students cannot be stressed enough. By choosing to get your MBA, you are increasing your influence throughout your network and society.

If you found this book useful, please share it with others. The worksheets and resources mentioned can be found at https://www.nextvets.com. Your feedback is always welcome.

ACKNOWLEDGEMENTS

It is impossible to include everyone and everything that influenced my thinking but know that I am humbled by the support I have received while writing this book.

I first want to thank my wife, Chelsea, for giving me the time I needed to complete this book. Your love, encouragement and selflessness helped me through the early mornings and late nights to complete this project as a full-time MBA student.

While I received feedback from many military veterans throughout the process, I would like to recognize a few individually:

- Ryan Bolles, for your manuscript edits and pushing me to clarify my thinking.
- Bryan Crosson, for your helpful comments and book -cover design concepts.
- Geordy Taylor, for your encouragement and help with the school NPV tool.
- Michael Hooper, for helping with the early concept and structure of the book.

I would also like to thank my classmates Adam Yoseph, Christopher Larsen and the entire NYU Stern veteran community for your encouragement and feedback.

Thank you to my professors Anat Lechner and Amy Webb. Anat, thanks for pushing me to think bigger. After hearing you say multiple times that I needed to digitize my efforts, I finally decided to write this book. Amy, thank you for being generous with your time and walking me through the pros and cons of the publishing process.

Last but not least is my copy editor, Phillip Blanchard. Your thoughtful commentary and meticulousness are what makes this book cohesive. Thank you.

ABOUT THE AUTHOR

Matthew Cowsert is a decorated U.S. Army veteran and veteran advocate. He received his undergraduate degree from The Citadel, The Military College of South Carolina in 2009. Matt spent seven years in the Army as an infantry and finance officer before earning his MBA at NYU Stern in 2018.

Matt also serves as the Director of Partnerships for the veteran non-profit Veterans in Global Leadership and is a Service to School MBA Ambassador. Matt will be working for Amazon as a Senior Product Manager in their Amazon Web Services organization.

Made in the USA
Middletown, DE
14 September 2019